Eyes
on the
Sky

Mars

by David M. Haugen

KidHaven Press

KidHaven Press, an imprint of Gale Group, Inc.
P.O. Box 289009, San Diego, CA 92198-9009

On cover: The *Mariner* probe in orbit around Mars.

Library of Congress Cataloging-in-Publication Data

Haugen, David M., 1969–
    Mars / by David M. Haugen.
      p. cm. — (Eyes on the sky)
    Includes bibliographical references.
    Summary: Discusses the scientific aspects of the planet
Mars, including its topographical makeup and the possibil-
ity that it may contain water and living things.
    ISBN 0-7377-0939-1 (hardback : alk. paper)
    1. Mars (Planet)—Juvenile literature. [1. Mars (Planet)] I.
Title.
    QB641 .H38 2002
    523.43—dc21

    2001003464

Picture Credits
Cover Photo: NASA
© AFP/CORBIS, 12, 20 (top right), 22, 23, 26, 28, 30, 31
© Bettmann/CORBIS, 35
© CORBIS, 15, 17, 20 (bottom), 29, 40
© Forrest J. Ackerman Collection/CORBIS, 34
© Lowell Georgia/CORBIS, 16, 37
Chris Jouan, 11
Chris Jouan and Martha Schierholz, 6–7
NASA, 9 (both), 39
© NASA/Roger Ressmeyer/CORBIS, 13, 18, 20 (top left), 25
© Reuters NewMedia Inc./CORBIS, 5
© James A. Sugar/CORBIS, 41

Copyright 2002 by KidHaven Press, an imprint of Gale Group, Inc.
P.O. Box 289009, San Diego, CA, 92198-9009

Printed in the U.S.A.

Table of Contents

1
A Closer Look at the Red Planet

The planet Mars is one of the few planets visible in the night sky. It stands out from other heavenly bodies because of its color. Mars is known as the red planet and, even to the unaided eye, its color shows up clearly. Mars was named after the Roman god of war, most likely because its reddish hue was connected with the bloody nature of warfare.

Mars has a red color because its surface is made up of rocks and soil rich in **iron oxide**, the same chemical compound that forms rust on Earth. Nearly the entire planet is covered by this rocky terrain, giving Mars a very uniform color. Because Mars is made up of rock, it is related to the three planets closest to the sun. These planets, Mercury, Venus, and

Earth, also have rocky surfaces. Because of this feature, they, along with Mars, are called the terrestrial planets. As the fourth planet from the sun, Mars is the last of the terrestrial planets. Beyond Mars lie the four gas giants—Saturn, Jupiter, Uranus, and Neptune—that are composed mostly of gas, and the tiny ice planet, Pluto.

A Small Planet with Weak Gravity

In size, Mars is much smaller than the huge gas giants, and a little smaller than Venus and Earth. The diameter—or distance across the

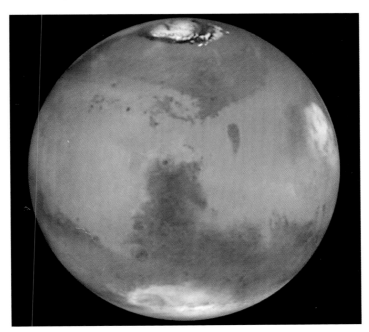

Mars takes its name from the Roman god of war.

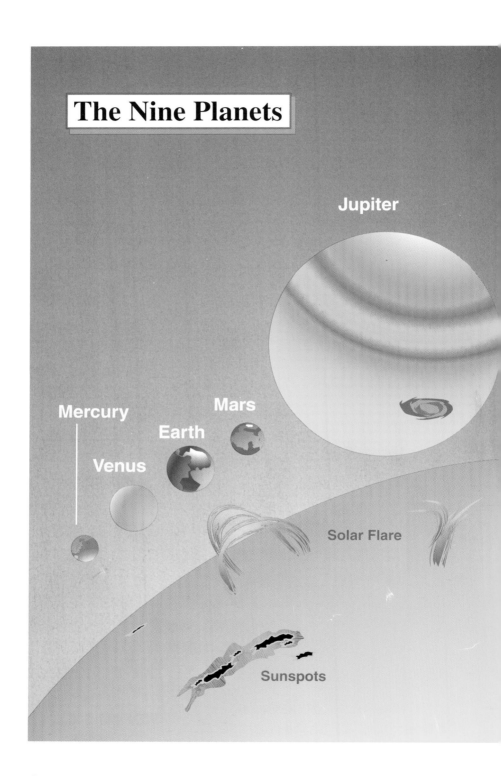

The Nine Planets

Jupiter

Mercury

Mars

Earth

Venus

Solar Flare

Sunspots

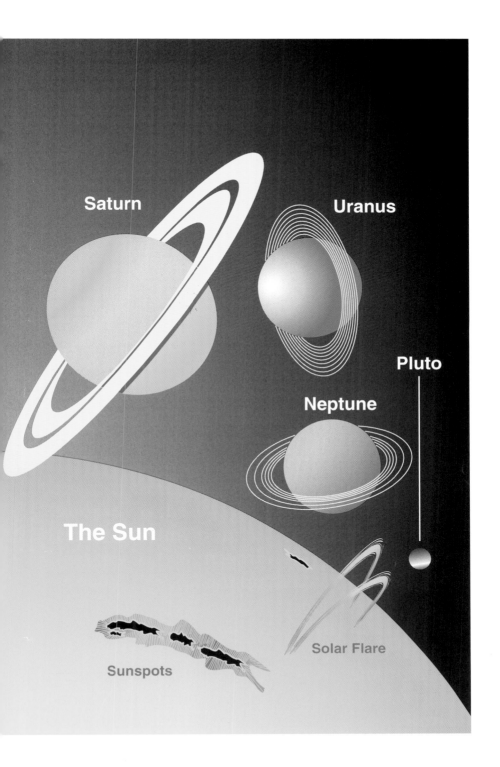

Saturn

Uranus

Pluto

Neptune

The Sun

Solar Flare

Sunspots

middle—of Mars is 4,222 miles. That's about half the size of Earth's diameter. Because Mars is smaller than Earth, the **gravity** on Mars is weaker than the gravity on Earth. Gravity is a force of attraction, and on the surface of a planet, gravity gives objects their weight. The weaker gravity on Mars means that things weigh less than they do on Earth. For example, an average adult weighing 150 pounds on Earth would weigh only 57 pounds on the Martian surface.

The weak gravity is also responsible for the lack of a thick, dense atmosphere on Mars. Earth's gravity has held its atmosphere tightly in place since the creation of the solar system. However, after Mars was formed, its weaker gravity allowed most of the gases that made up its atmosphere to float off into space. This explains why the atmosphere around Mars is so thin. More than 95 percent of its atmosphere is composed of **carbon dioxide** (the gas people and animals expel when they breathe); nitrogen, argon, oxygen, and water vapor make up the other 5 percent.

Phobos and Deimos

Although Mars has weak gravity, the force of attraction is strong enough to hold two moons in **orbit** around the planet. Called Deimos and Phobos, these two moons closely orbit—or trace a path around—Mars. Deimos circles Mars at a distance of 14,600 miles. Phobos is much closer, orbiting at only 5,829 miles from the Martian surface. In comparison, Earth's moon orbits at a distance of nearly 239,000 miles. Because its gravitational pull does not extend far from the planet, Mars could not possibly hold a moon in orbit at such a great distance.

Phobos and Deimos are very small moons. Unlike Earth's moon, they look like odd-shaped rocks. Phobos measures 6 miles by 7 miles by 10 miles, and Deimos, the larger of the two, measures 12.5 miles by 14 miles by 17 miles. Both have collided with **meteorites** many times throughout their lifetimes, and their surfaces are covered with impact craters.

Mars has two very small moons, Phobos (left) and Deimos (right).

 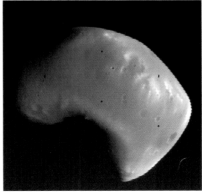

While held in orbit, Deimos circles Mars once every thirty-one hours. Because Phobos is much closer to Mars, it completes one orbit in just under eight hours. Astronomers think that Mars's gravity is causing an increase in Phobos's orbital speed. They predict that with an increased speed and the gravitational pull of Mars, Phobos will circle closer and closer to the planet until it crashes into the Martian surface. However, because the moon's speed is increasing only slightly over time, the collision won't happen for another 100 million years.

Mars's Elliptical Orbit

As the Martian moons circle the planet, Mars itself traces an orbit around the sun. Compared with Earth, Mars travels much slower in its orbit. It takes 687 Earth days for Mars to make one complete revolution around the sun, which is almost twice as long as it takes Earth to make the same trip. The path Mars follows as it orbits the sun is also quite different from that of Earth. While Earth orbits the sun in a nearly perfect circle, Mars's orbit looks more like a flattened circle called an ellipse. The elliptical path means that Mars's distance from the sun is not always constant. On its nearest approach, Mars is 129 million miles from the sun. When it is farthest away, it is 155 million miles from the sun.

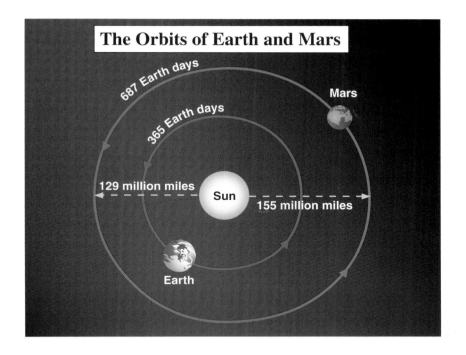

The Orbits of Earth and Mars

687 Earth days

365 Earth days

Mars

129 million miles

Sun

155 million miles

Earth

The Martian Climate

Because Mars is farther away from the sun than Earth is, temperatures on Mars are cooler than those on Earth. Summer temperatures at the Martian equator are around 70 degrees Fahrenheit. During the winter, the polar regions can reach nearly 220 degrees below zero. Mars experiences seasons just as Earth does. However, because it takes Mars almost twice as long to orbit the sun, the seasons last twice as long as those on Earth. Martian seasons are also unusual because they have large temperature changes. Since the distance between Mars and the sun changes as the planet orbits, the temperatures during a Martian winter or summer can rise and fall by as much as 85 degrees.

The changing temperatures also result in an unusual climate on Mars. During warm parts of a season, dust from the rocky surface often gets swept into the air by wind currents. Because of the weak gravity, these dust storms can stay in the Martian atmosphere for many days, and they spread out over huge sections of the planet—big enough to cover entire continents on Earth. When the temperatures cool as the planet moves away from the

Dust storms often block views of Mars (left) but not Earth (right).

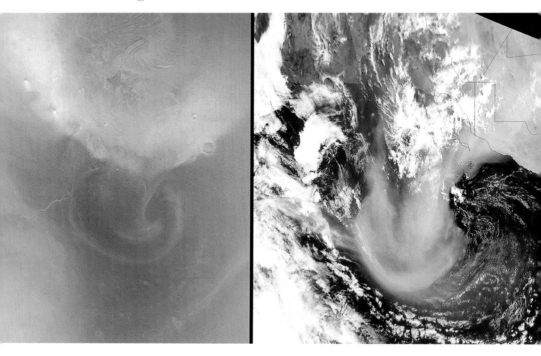

The Hubble telescope (pictured) gives astronomers a clear picture of the Martian landscape.

sun, water vapor in the atmosphere begins to freeze, forming huge ice clouds. These clouds block the sunlight, and the dust freezes in the atmosphere and falls back to the surface. As Mars passes close to the sun again on the other arc of its orbit, the clouds will melt away and the dust storms will return.

Mars Up Close

The wild weather patterns on Mars often block views of the planet from Earth. But the huge Hubble telescope that floats in space and probes that have landed on the Martian surface have given astronomers a clearer picture of the landscape hidden beneath the dust storms and ice clouds of Mars.

2
The Martian Surface

In 1965, the *Mariner 4* spacecraft became the first probe to make a successful pass by the planet Mars. The National Aeronautics and Space Administration (NASA) had equipped *Mariner 4* with television cameras to get close-up views of the Martian landscape. For centuries, astronomers had guessed at what the surface of the red planet would look like. Because Mars is a neighbor of Earth and because it is similar in size, rotation period, and even the angle at which it is tilted on its axis, scientists believed the planet might have a lush and livable surface like Earth. The twenty-two images from *Mariner*'s cameras presented a different picture. Mars was a barren planet with a rocky landscape dotted with deep craters. The surface reminded observers of the moon, not of the fertile Earth.

Over the next few years, other *Mariner* spacecraft headed toward Mars. None of these sent back clear images of the planet's surface. Only in 1971 when *Mariner 9* was sent directly into orbit around Mars did the mysteries of the planet's terrain begin to unfold. As *Mariner 9* circled Mars, it sent back seven thousand images of the planet showing details of 85 percent of the Martian surface. Most of the planet looked very much like the region *Mariner 4* photographed, but new features

Photographs from *Mariner 4* (pictured) showed that Mars is a barren, rocky planet.

such as huge volcanoes and deep canyons were also revealed. Five years later, NASA set two probes on the surface. *Viking 1* and *Viking 2* surveyed the landscape from ground level and also took soil samples. The images from these probes gave astronomers a much clearer idea of the geography of Mars.

A full-scale model of the Mars Viking lander shows its mechanical arm collecting soil samples.

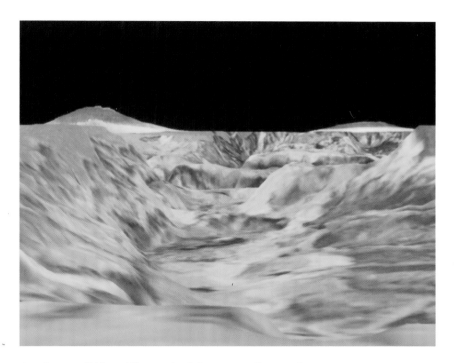

A view of the *Tharsis Montes*, the volcano region in the northern half of Mars.

Volcanoes on Mars

One feature of the Martian landscape stands out above all others. Located in the northern half of the planet are four giant volcanoes. Astronomers named these volcanoes Olympus Mons, Ascraeus Mons, Pavonis Mons, and Arsia Mons. They are taller than any mountains on Earth.

The four peaks lie in a chain along a ridge just above the planet's **equator**. Each has a broad base with sloping sides that reach up to a huge crater. Ascraeus, Pavonis, and Arsia are very large, with bases ranging between 190 and 250 miles wide. Olympus Mons, however, is the largest of all of them. The base of this volcano is 435 miles wide and is ringed by a steep cliff wall that is more than a mile in height. The low, flat cone rises to a point 16 miles above the ground. That is more than two and a half times the height of Mount Everest, the tallest mountain on Earth. In fact, Olympus Mons is the tallest known volcano in the **solar system**.

Olympus Mons, the tallest volcano in the solar system, stands sixteen miles high.

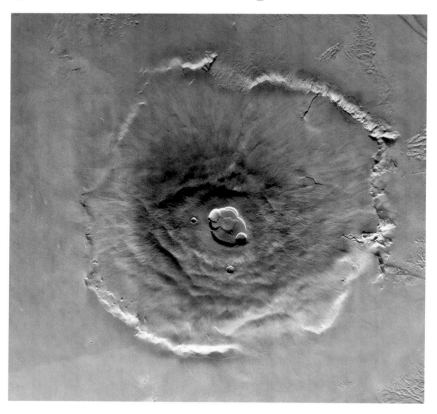

The volcanoes on Mars are not active. However, scientists say the landscape around them shows that the planet long ago had a lot of volcanic activity. That activity probably lasted many hundreds of millions of years and played a part in forming the planet. Surrounding the four main peaks is a big bubble which was formed by molten forces below the surface and lava flows that erupted from the volcanoes. This dome-shaped area is called the Tharsis region. It stretches for thousands of miles in all directions and rises about four miles above the rest of the Martian landscape.

The Great Canyons

Running eastward from the eastern edge of the Tharsis region is a series of canyons that extend along the planet's equator. The canyons are not as deep as the neighboring volcanoes are tall, but they are just as impressive. In some places, the huge canyons span 125 miles across and run up to 4 miles deep. Even some of the smallest canyons can hold Earth's Grand Canyon easily.

The canyon region is called Valles Marineris, or the Mariner Valley. It is named for the *Mariner 9* probe that sent the first images of the canyons back to Earth. From space, the long rift that forms the canyons is

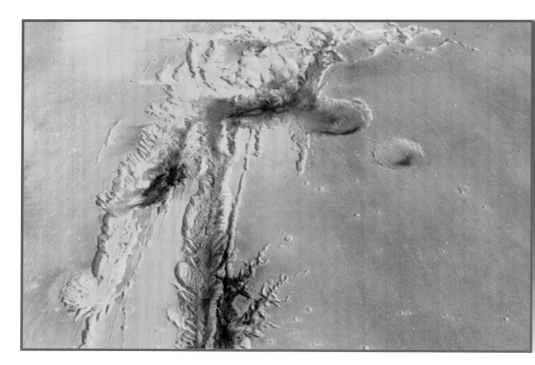

Three views of Valles Marineris, which spans three thousand miles.

not hard to see. It extends about three thousand miles, or nearly one-fifth of the way around the planet. Astronomers believe the giant canyons formed when tremendous forces pushed up and split the ground in the Tharsis region.

The Southern Plains

The Valles Marineris appears to be the dividing line between two very different types of Martian terrain. The northern half of Mars has many volcanic peaks. The southern half, on the other hand, has large stretches of flat plains dotted with many craters. The craters resulted from meteors that struck the planet when it was newly formed. Images from probes show hundreds of craters grouped near or overlapping each other. Scientists say the pattern of the craters suggests an intense bombardment of meteors in the early days of the solar system.

An Important Clue

The craters that make up the pockmarked surface of Mars have some unusual features. Most meteor craters look like hollow bowls surrounded by rings of ridges where the ground rippled after impact. The effect is similar to the pattern of rings that forms when a stone is dropped in water. On Mars, however, the ground does not form neat rings around the craters. Instead, it appears as if the surrounding land oozed away like mud, leaving a skirt of odd-shaped land flows around each crater.

Scientists call these unique Martian features "splosh craters." The name seems to imitate the sound the liquid earth made when it was struck by a heavy meteor. The sound and the name suggest that the ground may have

The "Happy Face" crater is one of many craters found on the planet's pockmarked surface.

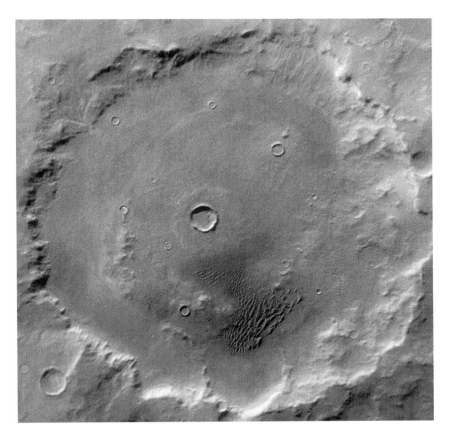

The land around a "splosh crater" looks like oozing mud.

been damp billions of years ago. Indeed, many scientists believe that a layer of water, ice, or another liquid entirely may have once existed just below the surface of the planet. It is very likely, then, that the Martian surface may not have always been as barren as it is now.

3
Is There Water on Mars?

In 1877, an Italian astronomer named Giovanni Schiaparelli turned his telescope on Mars. Schiaparelli began sketching what he saw through the lens: a series of connected lines that looked like scratches in the planet's surface. Other astronomers had seen light and dark patches on Mars before, but none had ever reported seeing this feature. Schiaparelli called his discovery *canali*, the Italian word for channels. Soon other scientists recorded sightings of *canali* on the planet, often increasing the number of lines. When newspapers eventually got hold of the news, some reporters mistakenly translated the word *canali* into the English word *canals*. The error had a lasting effect. Many people, including some scientists, saw the canals as a sign of intelligent life and water on Mars.

Looking for Canals and Finding Channels

Even after the announcement of Schiaparelli's discovery, not all astronomers who looked at

A photograph taken from outer space shows features that look like canals.

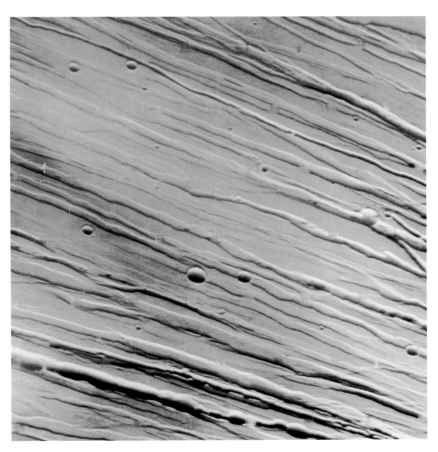

Mars through telescopes could see signs of lines or canals. These scientists assumed that the lines were imaginary; that is, they only appeared to people who wanted to believe that life existed on Mars. This controversy raged for nearly a hundred years before NASA took the first close-up pictures of Mars with the *Mariner 9* space probe.

Mariner's photographs showed no traces of canals on Mars. The lines Schiaparelli and others had seen were most likely caused by an unusual pattern created by the light and a desire to find signs of life on Mars. *Mariner* did reveal

Photos from *Mariner* expose channels carved by flowing water.

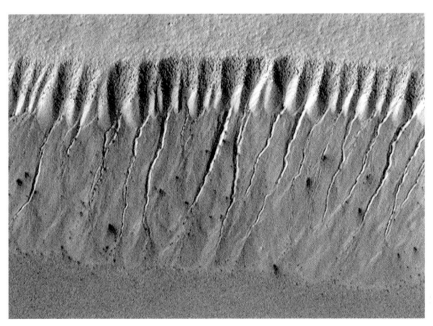

a startling discovery, however. Images showed low troughs and channels in the planet's northern regions. The troughs angle downward from the slopes of the raised plateaus that make up the highlands. Astronomers say that only a flowing liquid could have carved the land in this manner. Scientists now had evidence that water had once flowed on Mars.

Only Traces Remain

The water that once flowed on the Martian surface was also responsible for shaping many of the canyons in the Valles Marineris region of the planet. Although it did not create these huge rifts, rushing water played a major part in eroding the canyon walls and widening the gaps to their present size. Surging water also dug out many of the smaller cracks that branch off from the larger canyons. Seen from above, these offshoots look like rivers on Earth with tiny streams striking out in all directions.

All of these riverbeds and canyons are now dry. Erosion patterns suggest that water has not been present on Mars for 4 billion years. Today, water could not exist on the surface because there is not enough pressure from the planet's thin atmosphere to stop water from boiling away, even at temperatures below freezing. This suggests to scientists that Mars may have once had a thicker atmosphere, one that would allow water to stay on the planet's surface long enough to have carved the vast network of channels.

Evidence of running water on Mars answers one question but raises another. If there was once water on Mars, where did it come from? No one knows for sure. Scientists suspect that the volcanic forces that cracked the planet's surface and created the Valles Marineris may have released pockets of water that lay deep underground. Some scientists think there still is water in a frozen layer be-

Dry riverbeds suggest water once existed on Mars.

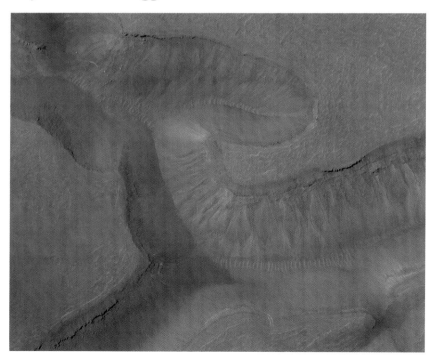

Ice-coated rocks might mean water exists below the Martian surface.

neath the Martian landscape. NASA's *Mars Global Surveyor*, a probe circling Mars and photographing the surface, has recently sent back images of what appear to be newer channels made by water being pushed up from an underground source. This may show that water is still moving somewhere within the planet. So far, however, the only evidence of water anywhere near the planet's surface is the ice locked up in the polar ice caps that sit at the northern and southern extremes of Mars.

Water at the Poles

Mars has large, white polar ice caps that stand out against the reddish color of the planet. Unlike the polar regions on Earth, the Martian ice caps are made up mainly of carbon dioxide gas from the atmosphere. At the low Martian temperatures, the carbon dioxide freezes into what is commonly called dry ice. The ice falls like snow and blankets the landscape for hundreds of miles.

During the winter months at each pole, the dry-ice layers can extend up to twelve hundred miles. In summer months, however, the temperatures along the edges of each cap will increase enough to turn the ice back into

During summer, the layer of dry ice at the south pole shrinks.

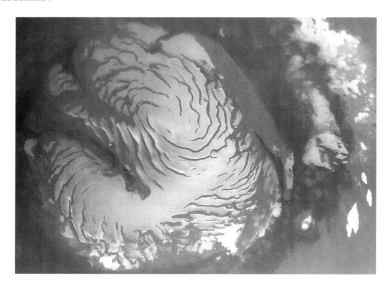

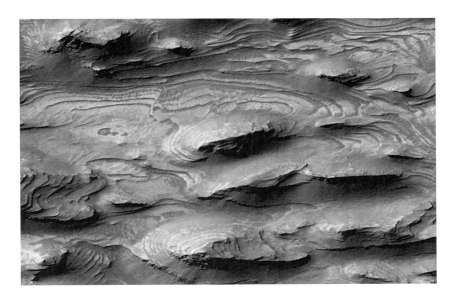

Scientists hope rock layers like these will reveal the secrets of Mars.

a gas. The south pole can lose as much as eleven hundred miles of its icy reach. The north pole, on the other hand, never loses more than nine hundred miles despite being subjected to similar heat.

Astronomers believe the north pole retains more of its frozen landscape during its summer months because the ice cap is made up of more than just dry ice. Although the summer temperatures would be high enough to evaporate carbon dioxide, they would not be above the freezing point of water. Therefore, under the winter blanket of *dry* ice is most likely a permanent layer of *water* ice. The water lying under these ice caps is the only water that scientists have seen on Mars. How long the water has been in these polar regions is unknown. Scientists hope that the water layers are old enough to hold bits of debris and dust from the eras when water flowed on the planet's surface. If they are, these ice caps may be a storehouse of Martian history waiting for some future Earth mission to uncover the secrets of the planet.

The Essence of Life

The evidence of water on the Martian surface interests astronomers because water is needed for life. It is possible that during the times when water rushed through the channels and canyons of Mars, some simple life-forms developed. Scientists believe the ice caps may still hold a record of some of these life-forms if they ever existed. Of course, water is only one of the conditions needed for life to form. Temperature and climate also matter. Conditions on Mars would have to have been very different than they are today for life to evolve. However, the presence and then disappearance of water in the Martian past suggests that some shifts in climate probably did take place at one time. Was this enough to start life on the cold, red planet? Several space missions have already been sent to Mars to try and answer that question.

4

The Search for Life on Mars

During the late 1800s, the legend of the canals of Mars sparked a great deal of interest in the possibility of life on the planet. Scientists and others wondered who could have built waterways so large that they could be seen from Earth. With no way of knowing, most people simply used their imaginations. They described all sorts of fantastic creatures, many of which looked human and had advanced technology. Some of these ideas worked their way into scientific essays and popular fiction.

"The Martians Are Coming!"

In the early 1900s, a type of writing called science fiction was born. Authors wrote adventure stories that were in part based on scientific knowledge. These fantastic tales seemed at least possible to some readers. Since people did not know a lot about other planets, they accepted some of the ideas in these stories as true.

One writer and actor named Orson Welles played upon the fear of a Martian invasion in a 1938 radio broadcast called *War of the Worlds*. Although this story of hostile Martians coming to Earth was adapted from an older novel, few listeners had read it or even heard of it before Welles's version hit the air. More importantly, Welles made his broadcast

The possibility of life on Mars fueled a new area of writing called science fiction.

A cartoon depicts Orson Welles's radio broadcast *War of the Worlds*.

sound as if the events he and his fellow radio actors described were actually happening at that time. *War of the Worlds* was designed to frighten audiences, but Welles did not know just how scared people would become. Actors pretending to be reporters where the aliens had landed in New Jersey screamed, "The Martians are coming!" Not realizing the broadcast was fictional, many listeners in the surrounding area panicked. Hundreds of people called the radio station to find out if the news they were hearing was true. Surveys done a week later found that nearly a million people believed Martians had invaded Earth.

The End of an Era

As astronomy improved over the next twenty years, scientists were able to learn a lot more about Mars. However, they still had no idea just what lay on the Martian surface. Since science could not prove or disprove the notion of Martian life, science fiction writing and even movies continued to populate the red planet with a host of weird aliens. It was not until the 1960s that nations such as Russia and the United States developed space programs which could send probes to Mars in hopes of answering the question of Martian life once and for all.

In 1965, the first *Mariner* spacecraft sent back its images of Mars, ending the nearly one-hundred-year-old controversy over the sightings of canals on the planet's surface. The cameras on board the craft revealed no traces of waterways, plants, or any kind of civilization. Over the next few years, as other *Mariner* probes mapped more of the planet, it became clear that advanced life-forms could not have existed on Mars.

Invisible Life?

If advanced life-forms had never existed on Mars, had some other, simpler life-forms ever been present? NASA set out to answer this question starting in 1976. In that year, *Viking 1* and *2* successfully touched down on Mars.

Landing more than forty-five hundred miles apart, the unmanned *Viking* probes immediately began taking soil samples. Laboratory instruments on board each probe tested the samples. Scientists on Earth were hopeful that one of the experiments would reveal the presence of tiny organisms called microbes within the Martian soil. After three different tests, however, the samples came up empty. In the ground around the craft, there was no trace of life.

A scientist examines soil collected from the Mars *Viking* probe.

Despite the negative results, astronomers knew that the *Viking* ships had taken samples from only two small sites on a huge planet. Perhaps life might be found in other parts of the planet. Perhaps simple life-forms existed deeper in the ground or under the frozen polar ice caps.

The Martian Meteorite

Although the *Viking* missions dimmed the hope of finding life on Mars, the search has not ended. About twenty years later, a new piece of evidence was brought to the attention of scientists. In 1996, a group of scientists published a story about a meteorite found in Antarctica twelve years before. The meteorite was 4.5 billion years old, and by analyzing the rock, the scientists determined that it had come to Earth from Mars. More importantly, within the rock the scientists found traces of **hydrocarbons**, elements left behind when organisms die. They also discovered what they believe are fossil remains of microscopic bacteria carved into the rock. Science was once again looking to the possibility of life on Mars.

The story on the Martian meteorite stirred up the old controversy. In the meantime, research continues. Many more tests

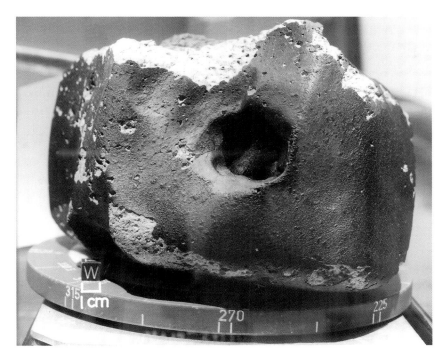

The Martian meteorite found in Antarctica reveals traces of once-living organisms also found on earth.

will have to be done before anyone can say for sure what these microscopic findings mean.

Not Giving Up Hope

In 1997, NASA's Mars *Pathfinder* mission placed another probe on the surface of Mars. As part of the mission, a small robotic rover equipped with a camera brought scientists new images of a small area of the Martian terrain. While the rover rolled over the planet's surface, the main probe conducted experiments with the soil just as *Viking* had done. And just like *Viking*, the *Pathfinder* probe was unable to turn up evidence of life.

Although it came up empty-handed, the *Pathfinder* mission showed that scientists are still unwilling to give up the search for life on Mars. Another probe was sent up in 1998. This one carried a landing craft to examine a polar region of the planet, with the hope that the water in the ice cap might be a more likely place to find living or dead organisms. Unfortunately, NASA lost touch with the spacecraft

An artist's version of the *Pathfinder* lander and a robotic rover (left) on Mars.

Scientists hope this and other rovers will bring home new information about Mars.

as it traveled through space. Still, NASA intends to send a probe with two more rovers to the Martian surface in 2003. Whether either of these will find evidence of life, no one can say. Yet one thing is sure: With each new mission to Mars, humankind's knowledge of the planet increases. Even if no traces of life are found, the 2003 rover mission—like *Viking* and *Pathfinder* before it—will bring science a little closer to unraveling the many remaining mysteries of the red planet.

Glossary

carbon dioxide: A gas that is not suitable for humans to breathe. Carbon dioxide is the main gas in the Martian atmosphere.

equator: An imaginary line that circles the middle of a planet, separating the northern half from the southern half.

gravity: The force of attraction. Gravity on Mars draws all matter to the surface of the planet.

hydrocarbons: Chemical elements in living things that do not disappear when the organisms die. Finding traces of hydrocarbons within the Martian soil may point to the existence of life on the planet.

iron oxide: The chemical compound present in the Martian soil that makes it look red. On Earth, iron oxide is another name for rust.

meteorite: A piece of rock from space that has fallen onto a planet's surface. Meteors have impacted against the surface of Mars and its moons, leaving behind craters.

orbit: The path of one heavenly body revolving around another. The revolving body is held in orbit partly by the gravity of the central body. This helps explain why an orbiting body continues to revolve around the central body instead of flying off into space.

solar system: The sun and the collection of planets, moons, and other smaller objects (such as asteroids) that revolve around it. Mars is the fourth planet from the sun.

For Further Exploration

Duncan Brewer, *Mars*. New York: Marshall Cavendish, 1992. A simple yet attractive book on Mars. It is filled with many pictures and illustrations.

Eric Burgess, *To the Red Planet*. New York: Columbia University Press, 1978. Although out of date, this book relates the compelling story of the *Viking* missions to Mars in great detail.

Martin Caidin and Jay Barbree, with Susan Wright, *Destination Mars: In Art, Myth, and Science*. New York: Penguin, 1997. This book examines how people have viewed Mars through the ages. From ancient myths of the war god to more recent paranoia over Martian invasions, the book covers a wide range of topics. Overall, it is a fun resource that ties fascinating facts to fanciful legends.

NASA Kids (http://kids.msfc.nasa.gov). This is the National Aeronautics and Space Administration's website designed especially for kids. It contains very basic information on the planets and many fun projects to try. The site is updated regularly with reports on the best times to view astronomical events as well as upcoming NASA projects.

The Near Planets. Alexandria, VA: Time-Life Books, 1989. An older but thorough study of Earth, Mars, Mercury, and Venus. The chapter on Mars discusses the missions to Mars and the basic facts about the planet. The book as a whole helps illustrate how the planets near the sun are related.

Gregory L. Vogt, *Mars*. Brookfield, CT: Millbrook Press, 1994. A basic guide to the red planet appropriate for young readers.

Index

About the Author

David M. Haugen edits books for Lucent Books and Greenhaven Press. He holds a master's degree in English literature and has also worked as a writer and instructor.